A Journey of Courage, Faith, and Hope

RUN TO WIN

ANNITA M. MANNINO

WESTBOW
P R E S S®
A DIVISION OF THOMAS NELSON
& ZONDERVAN

Scriptures taken from the Holy Bible, New International Version®, NIV®.
Copyright © 1973, 1978, 1984, 2011 by Biblica, Inc.™ Used by permission
of Zondervan. All rights reserved worldwide. www.zondervan.com The
"NIV" and "New International Version" are trademarks registered in
the United States Patent and Trademark Office by Biblica, Inc.™

WestBow Press books may be ordered through booksellers or by contacting:

WestBow Press
A Division of Thomas Nelson & Zondervan
1663 Liberty Drive
Bloomington, IN 47403
www.westbowpress.com
1 (866) 928-1240

Because of the dynamic nature of the Internet, any web addresses or
links contained in this book may have changed since publication and
may no longer be valid. The views expressed in this work are solely those
of the author and do not necessarily reflect the views of the publisher,
and the publisher hereby disclaims any responsibility for them.

Any people depicted in stock imagery provided by Getty Images are
models, and such images are being used for illustrative purposes only.
Certain stock imagery © Getty Images.

ISBN: 978-1-9736-3988-6 (sc)
ISBN: 978-1-9736-3989-3 (hc)
ISBN: 978-1-9736-3987-9 (e)

Library of Congress Control Number: 2018911837

Print information available on the last page.

WestBow Press rev. date: 11/14/2018

To all mothers who walk a journey.
May God pick you up and carry you through!

I am forever grateful to my parents, Sam and Annita Cracchiolo, for the spiritual foundation they instilled in my life at such an early age. For without that, life's valleys would be impossible.

To my husband, Tom. Through Christ, we walk together down the path that has been laid out before us.

To Tommy and Andrea. May David always be a testimony to you, and may his faith and courage always be present in your hearts.

For David

I press on toward the goal to win the prize for which God has called me heavenward in Christ Jesus.

—Philippians 3:14

Angelic in innocence, incorruptible in faith, a boy who could climb any mental mountain and a man who could carry the weak through valleys of despair. He passed through the thickets of disbelief, clearing a path, clean and unblemished by indecision, a path that demands courage and resolve one for all to trek, a path that reaches far beyond the superficial delights and into the eternal and cerebral satisfaction of faith. David carved a path and stands as a pillar, a landmark of righteousness by which we may gauge our own proximity to the bravery, to a path that he cut. He is loved now and always as everything I hope to become. A man carried by a whimsical faith, unblemished by the snares of the wicked, grounded in a true and present God.

—James Peterson, friend of David

This is a testimony of an eighteen-year-old boy who not only loved life and family and exemplified incredible faith and love for the Lord but also demonstrated a courage that only could have come from God Himself—a courage that carried him through a seven-month journey that touched the lives of many and continues to teach by example.

Be strong and courageous. Do not be afraid; do not be discouraged, for the Lord your God will be with you wherever you go.

—Joshua 1:9

Chapter 1

Springtime in the Midwest is always welcomed after the flurry of winter has been laid to rest. The robins lay their eggs, flowers bud, and trees bloom, while pollen blows gently across the fields. The sun finally shines through the windows, bringing anticipated warmth.

That's how it was on the evening of May 3, 2011: a perfect spring night. We had just finished dinner, and David excused himself from the table, only to turn around and look at his father and me and state, "Oh, by the way, I have a lump in my neck."

I had no idea that those seven words would begin an all-consuming journey. I had no idea that at that very moment, David's entire future would be rerouted.

It is my desire that God will speak through these pages to bring courage, hope, and healing to those experiencing a challenging journey themselves.

> Therefore, in order to keep me from becoming conceited, I was given a thorn in my flesh, a messenger of Satan, to torment me. Three times I pleaded with the Lord to take it away from

me. But he said to me, "My grace is sufficient for you, for my power is made perfect in weakness." Therefore, I will boast all the more gladly about my weaknesses, so that Christ's power may rest on me. That is why for Christ's sake I delight in weaknesses, in insults, in hardships, in persecutions, in difficulties. For when I am weak, then I am strong. (2 Corinthians 12:7–10)

David was the third child born to Tom and me and the baby of our family. He was five to six years younger than his siblings, Tommy and Andrea. At times, it felt like he was an only child. David was raised in a Christian household and attended a Christian high school, the University of Detroit Jesuit. His journey started just fourteen days before his high school graduation. We were looking forward to that day, which would be the last high school graduation for the Mannino family. Not only did David earn a 4.2 GPA and many senior academic awards, but his spot at the University of Michigan was also secure. David was scheduled to attend U of M in the fall as a pre-med student. His deep desire was to help those in need, and studying medicine was his ultimate goal.

A close second to medicine was his love for sports, especially hockey. David was an ice shoveler for the Detroit Red Wings. During TV time-outs, David would skate across the ice, shoveling off any excess ice that had built up while the players were skating. Oftentimes, octopuses were thrown onto the ice by the fans after a goal was scored. That was a tradition at Joe Louis Arena, and David's additional job was to remove and dispose of them.

David removing an octopus off the ice at Joe
Louis Arena during a Red Wings hockey game

But back to that spring night. David said to me, "Mom, do you
think it could be cancer?"

"Absolutely not!" I responded.

How could a "healthy," active, strong boy getting ready to graduate
from high school, with his *future* on the horizon, have cancer?

"No, not possible!" I stated.

But just to alleviate his fears and mine at that point, I told David
that I would take him in to be seen by our doctor.

After school the following day, Wednesday, May 4, 2011, I took
David to see our primary care physician, who explained that David

needed bloodwork and a CAT scan. I remember thinking, *A CAT scan for what? Swollen lymph nodes? How can this be?*

My mind was swirling with confusion, but David remained calm. The CAT scan was scheduled for the next day, and by Friday, we were at the oncologist's office. He informed us that, although there was a slim chance that this could be nothing, more than likely it was Hodgkin's lymphoma. The oncologist explained that should this diagnosis be accurate, Hodgkin's lymphoma was very treatable and would require four to six months of chemotherapy. However, to be sure of the exact diagnosis, a biopsy of the lump would be in order. Surgery was scheduled for the following Wednesday.

That car ride home from the oncologist's office that afternoon was extremely quiet. We were all too stunned and numb to have idle conversation. Wednesday would come soon enough, and the uncertainty would be answered.

After several minutes of no conversation, David, sitting in the backseat, announced, "Mom and Dad, if something happens to me and I don't survive this, promise me that you will never lose your faith."

From that moment on, David steadfastly resisted any negative thoughts and only forged ahead with God and his faith in the driver's seat.

> Look to the Lord and His strength; seek His face always. (Psalm 105:4)

Right there, in the backseat, David became an ambassador for Christ. His testimony was birthed. Nothing, *absolutely nothing,* would rob him of his joy for life and his faith in Christ—not even a potential cancer diagnosis.

> I pledge to stand fearless in the face of adversity
> and bring it every day.
> —David Mannino, May 7, 2011, Facebook post

That weekend, before his surgery, was one of the longest weekends of our lives. We tried to stay as busy as possible and spent most of the time with family and friends as we all waited to learn whether that tiny lump, which appeared to be so harmless on the surface, would prove to be detrimental.

We later learned through the CAT scan results that David was affected with abnormal cells throughout his lymphatic system.

Meanwhile, David's love for hockey was a great distraction. The Detroit Red Wings were in the Stanley Cup playoffs and played the night before his surgery. Normally, David would have shoveled the ice during that game, but due to his surgery in the morning, he sat out and watched on TV. It was not quite the same as being there, but David took the win anyway. And watching his favorite team play helped to take the focus off the next day's biopsy.

> The boys won game six for me, and now my game
> begins ... Time to bring it!
> —David Mannino, May 11, 2011, day of surgery,
> Facebook post

Surgery went well. The lump on his neck was removed, and the real waiting game began.

> Just got out of surgery ... Brought it like I never
> have before!
> —David Mannino, May 11, 2011, Facebook post

We were so thankful for all the family and friends who showed up at the hospital to support and love David. As a parent, this was my worst nightmare. Watching my seventeen-year-old child standing at the precipice of life, waiting to embark on a bright future—a future filled with dreams, hopes, and plans—only to hear the words in my head, *Not so fast! He may be derailed!* I can't even put into words or describe the ache in the pit of my stomach. I thought, *God, is this for real? Is this really happening to my child, to my family, and to me?*

> Many are the plans in a person's heart, but it is the Lord's purpose that prevails. (Proverbs 19:21)

> Well simply put, God has given me an unexpected enemy, and now I need to bring everything I have.
> —David Mannino, May 11, 2011, Facebook post

While David was in recovery from the surgery, his first post-anesthesia experience was anything but serene. He was so loopy and giddy that he had all the nurses in laughter. David had a fabulous sense of humor and would draw a crowd even in the most unusual circumstances. Even with an ominous outcome looming, he never lost his joy or ability to make people laugh. In fact, David loved the field of medicine so much that he never feared medical procedures and doctors. He was accustomed to needle pokes because he had required frequent blood draws ever since birth since he had been born without a thyroid gland and needed his thyroid levels checked often.

Before we left the hospital, the oncologist informed us that as soon as any results came through he would call us, even if they were only preliminary. Thus, we anxiously drove home and waited to see what the future would hold.

Later that afternoon, Tommy came over to the house to sit with us. Andrea had left two days earlier for Israel on a missions trip. We all just tried to go about our afternoon as usual, but not really! David was upstairs in his room, while Tom, Tommy, and I were talking in the family room.

Around 5:30 p.m., Tom's cell phone rang. It was the doctor! Tom got up off the couch and started talking low so that David wouldn't hear and become alarmed, but David could clearly hear.

Tom's face became pale with disbelief, and the pitch in his voice began to change. It wasn't Hodgkin's lymphoma. It was worse! David had non-Hodgkin's—acute lymphoblastic lymphoma (ALL)—and the treatment would be two years of chemotherapy.

At that moment, I stood up, only to collapse. Just as I hit the floor, David came downstairs and stood over me. He had heard every word.

He calmly and sternly looked at me and said, "Get up. Don't we serve a greater God than this? You need to be strong for me. Now get up. We will get through this."

Not one tear even rolled from his eyes. I could not speak. I stood up and threw my arms around him and sobbed. There were no words. There was only intense heartache and grief. *How do I console my son?* For seventeen years, I was able to mend any cut, scrape, or mishap, but cancer? David consoled me!

From that moment on, David became my teacher, my teacher of the faith. He showed me that faith isn't what you believe God can do for you. Faith is believing in the personality of who God is and trusting in His decisions, not ours.

> Now faith is confidence in what we hope for and
> assurance about what we do not see. (Hebrews 11:1)

David's diagnosis passed through the hands of God.

> The Lord has established His throne in the
> heavens; and His sovereignty rules over all.
> (Psalm 103:19)

Just prior to David's surgery, I had informed the dean of his high
school that David would not be in attendance for his final exams,
which were scheduled for the following week. Graduation was set
for May 17, 2011. The dean was incredibly shocked to hear this
news but sympathetically excused David from all of his exams and
stated that David, who had all A's throughout his four years, was
officially finished with high school. No exams were needed. David
had enough to worry about. David had completed high school!

Chapter 2

News of David's diagnosis spread quickly among family and friends. That very evening some of David's aunts, uncles, and cousins came over to lend their support. In an Italian family, news, whether good or bad, travels extremely fast. In this case, it was a blessing. With that kind of diagnosis, there were so many questions and concerns that having others to lean on was comforting. Our primary care physician, who was a family friend, had stopped over to talk to David as well, and then the thought occurred to me that I would have to call Andrea in Israel, as she too was waiting for results. That missions trip had been planned for months, but when all of this transpired with David, Andrea wanted to cancel. I told her to continue with her plans and I would inform her by phone of all the necessary information. Later that evening, I went into a quiet room and placed that call. Andrea, of course, was deeply saddened to hear that her brother had a cancer diagnosis. The fact that it was an even worse type of cancer than originally thought made it all the more difficult to comprehend. Andrea shared the news with the other people on that missions team, and prayers were immediately given up on David's behalf. At that moment, Andrea's missions trip took on a whole new meaning for her—a pilgrimage.

That night, no one slept well in the Mannino household. We were in such shock over this distressing news that we felt dazed, almost immobilized. However, David remained calm and resolute. He was a very cerebral thinker. As long as he was provided with all the information, he was able to internalize it and remain focused. His faith in a sovereign God, his ability to deeply meditate on each moment, and thoroughly research every step of the way would become his coping mechanisms.

> Through God I believe that I will win and stand firm in the face of adversity! I have only one thing to say to my adversary—just bring it!
> —David Mannino, May 12, 2011, Facebook post

The very next morning, Tom started making phone calls to various hospitals locally and across the country. What was the protocol in treating ALL, and where would be the best place for treatment? We were instructed that David needed a bone marrow biopsy. We needed to learn if there was any involvement of cancer cells in David's bone marrow. That morning, Thursday, May 12, I took David back to the hospital, and the bone marrow biopsy was performed. Within a few hours we learned that in fact there was a 10 percent involvement, indicating that David had leukemia as well (lymphoma/leukemia). I felt like I had just been slapped across the face for the second time!

David knew the battle was to begin. No matter what God should allow, David carried with him the strength of the Lord. He submitted to God's will and never questioned his journey. "Why me?" did not exist.

> When you pass through the waters I will be with you, and when you pass through the rivers, they will not sweep over you. When you walk through the fire, you will not be burned; the flames will not

set you ablaze. For I am the Lord your God, the
holy one of Israel. (Isaiah 43:2–3)

The following morning, Friday, May 13, David, Tom and I drove
back to the hospital. A decision needed to be made now that we
had a definitive diagnosis. Should he be treated locally or out
of state? We met with a couple of oncologists, who both agreed
that David should be treated at the pediatric level. Even though
David was one month from turning eighteen and six foot two,
it was strongly suggested that we treat at the pediatric level due
to the intensity of the chemotherapy and better success rate for
young adults. Upon conferring with several pediatric oncologists
from various institutions, we learned that the treatment for ALL
would be directed from the COG (children's oncology group)
and that all the hospitals would be following the same protocol.
Therefore, we decided to stay local. We chose one of our hometown
hospitals. David wanted the love and support of family and friends
around him.

> Well, I'm staying home! Fight begins Monday.
> Gonna bring it 100 percent.
> –David Mannino, May 13, 2011, Facebook post

David's friends were flooding our house. I had never seen so many
young adults ringing my doorbell. The love they showed David and
the concern they had for him will forever be in our hearts. This
sudden event in David's life completely challenged the priorities
of each one of those teens. The innocence of youth was harshly
met with the cruel reality of life. This was something that none of
them were prepared for and had never experienced. The support of
these friends would be instrumental in David's healing, and David
became an example of courage and faith to all of them.

Chapter 3

When choosing a high school for David, there was no dilemma, for the University of Detroit Jesuit was the only choice. University of Detroit is an all-boys Catholic high school in Detroit, Michigan. This renowned high school was founded in 1877. Not only did David receive an outstanding education there, but he also played on the varsity hockey team. Their motto, "*Ad Majorem Dei Gloriam*" (for the greater glory of God) and slogan, "Men For Others," was reflected in the young men they graduated. As is customary for most Catholic high schools, a baccalaureate mass at the end of the senior year honors the graduating seniors. Sunday, May 15, 2011, was the baccalaureate mass for David's class. That was the day before David would begin chemotherapy. On Saturday, May 14, the day before the mass, I received a phone call from one of the mothers of another graduating senior. She suggested that David should receive his diploma at the end of that mass and that she was going to contact the principal to make the appropriate arrangements. I was beyond elated to think that, regardless of the circumstances, David would formally receive what he had worked so hard for. The principal, who thought it was a great idea, sent out an email to many families, making the announcement. The church where the mass was held, St. Peter and Paul Catholic Church, was filled beyond capacity. The occasion turned out to be a very moving and special moment for David and our family. The front row was reserved for us, along with some of the other boys. At the end of the mass, the principal walked up to the altar and explained that he had a special announcement. He acknowledged David's academic achievements and disclosed that David would not be at graduation, as he would be in the hospital beginning chemotherapy treatments. He called David to the altar, and he, along with the priest performing the mass, presented David with his diploma. At that moment every student who played hockey and all of his closest buddies rushed onto the altar and surrounded him, cheering him on. Needless to say, there wasn't a dry eye in the house. There are no words to explain the level of emotion that was felt at that very moment. Something so sweet came from something so unexpected. What a sendoff on that day, the day before his journey would begin.

David recieves his diploma with high honors at the Baccalaureate Mass along side his proud parents.

Classmates rush to the alter to be pictured with
David (top-center) at Saints Peter and Paul
Jesuit Catholic Church, Detroit, Michigan.

Fight starts tomorrow.
—David Mannino, May 15, 2011, Facebook post

Thanks to everyone at the mass! Tomorrow the
battle begins, and with your help and with the
power of God, we will all bring it together and win.
—David Mannino, May 15, 2011, Facebook post

A great person sent this to me: "you gain strength,
courage, and confidence by every experience in
which you really stop to look fear in the face."
—Eleanor Roosevelt

Tomorrow I look fear in the face and will bring everything I got. Good night to all and thanks for everything! Tomorrow the battle begins. Team Bring It rolls at 100 percent tomorrow. Let's bring it!

—David Mannino, May 15, 2011, Facebook post

Chapter 4

Monday morning, May 16, 2011, we got up early and headed to the hospital. As previously mentioned, the protocol for treating ALL was two years of chemotherapy. The first nine months were intended to be very intense. The remaining fifteen months would be at a maintenance level. Because of the duration of treatment, we decided that placing a port surgically was the best option. A port is used in treating cancer patients so that the patient's vein is more accessible for injections of medications, blood transfusions, and administration of antibiotics and other fluids. David's port was placed in his upper left chest area. We arrived at the hospital by 7:00 a.m., and David went directly to pre-op. By the time surgery was completed and the port placed, it was approaching 11:00 a.m. From recovery he was wheeled to the fifth floor of the pediatric unit, room 5355, where we were met by a kind and loving floor nurse. She looked at David and greeted him as if he was her best friend. She instantly bonded with him, and I knew David would be comfortable. She even looked over at me and must have read the fear and anxiety that was all over my face.

"We give moms hugs here!" she stated.

Thank God! Because quite honestly, I thought I was going to faint. This dream, which was more like a nightmare, was now a reality.

So much had transpired in so few days. It's funny how you plan and think you've got everything in order and in one heartbeat those plans change. Lord help me!

> All the days ordained for me were written in your
> book before one of them came to be. (Psalm 139:16)

> Why, you do not even know what will happen
> tomorrow. What is your life? You are a mist that
> appears for a little while and then vanishes.
> (James 4:14)

Immediately following that initial welcoming, Dr. Gregory, one of the pediatric oncologists, walked into David's room with Susan. Susan was a pediatric oncology nurse. She was not a floor nurse but a nurse who worked exclusively with the pediatric oncologists. She was aware of all that was going on and kept all the doctors on task and organized. She was valued by all of them and greatly relied upon. She was immensely knowledgeable on all aspects of pediatric cancer. Susan truly loved what she did, and it showed. She connected with each patient and made them feel secure. Susan loved David's wit and precociousness. A special relationship was forged between David, Susan, and our family. I immediately felt a sense of security knowing that Susan would be there each day to watch over David. Susan was not just an incredible nurse, but she was a mother as well, and she truly understood the needs of those patients who were so young. God had totally given us an angel.

> And my God will meet all your needs according
> to the riches of his glory in Christ Jesus.
> (Philippians 4:19)

Susan explained that before the initial dose of chemotherapy, she and Dr. Gregory would go over the entire two-year plan. They indicated that this first hospital admission would last approximately two weeks. At that moment, I couldn't even think. I felt paralyzed with anxiety. How could I comprehend all that was about to take place? Susan handed me a white binder that was several inches thick. Everything I would need to know would be contained in that binder, and she and Dr. Gregory would verbally explain each stage of the treatment. Talk about overwhelming!

Susan gently stated, "Don't worry. As the doctor speaks, I will take notes for you."

With that, a notebook opened, and Susan began writing. Thank God, because my head started swirling. I was under the illusion that David would receive only one type of chemotherapy for that two-year duration of time. I couldn't have been more wrong. Dr. Gregory went on to explain that the protocol for ALL was broken down into five stages:

1. Induction—inducing remission (one month)
2. Consolidation—working on the central nervous system (approximately two months)
3. Interim maintenance—six to eight weeks
4. Delayed intensification—"knockout punch for lymphoma" (approximately eight weeks)
5. Maintenance—remainder of treatment (supposedly during this phase life would get back to "normal")

Dr. Gregory also explained each chemotherapy drug that would be given during each stage and potential side effects. He informed us that in the first stage there would be twenty-eight days of very high doses of prednisone, a steroid. Apparently, prednisone blasts lymphoid cells.

During all those stages, there would be a total of nine different types of chemotherapy agents administered through various means: oral, IV, intramuscular, and through the spinal fluid column.

The bone marrow is where all blood is produced. Red blood cells carry oxygen. White blood cells fight infection, and platelets aid in clotting. The doctors stated that in David's case, lymphoma/leukemia, it wasn't certain whether the cancer started in his lymph nodes or in his bone marrow. Both showed presence of disease, and that would require a strict protocol of chemotherapy treatments. To closely monitor David's blood levels, repeated blood tests and numerous hospital admissions, along with periodic bone marrow biopsies and spinal taps, would be in order. When blood counts might drop too low, a side effect of the chemotherapy, blood transfusions would be necessary. Unfortunately, chemotherapy targets not only diseased cells but healthy cells as well. By then my head was spinning, and a distressing anxiety was setting in. *Please, Lord, give me Your strength!*

> Truly he is my rock and my salvation; he is my fortress, I will never be shaken. (Psalm 62:12)

> Praise be to the God and father of our Lord Jesus Christ, the Father of compassion and the God of all comfort, who comforts us in all our troubles.
> (2 Corinthians 1:3–4)

Chapter 5

First chemo starts in approximately fifteen
minutes ... Team Bring It is ready to rumble.
—David Mannino, May 16, 2011, Facebook post

Dr. Gregory and Susan had finished their dissertation and left
the room. The first round of chemotherapy would begin, and
Susan would be the nurse to administer it. She walked back into
the room, gloves on, with Vincristine, the chemotherapy, in
hand. It was clearly labeled in a special clear plastic container.
She accessed David's port, and within minutes that first injection
of chemotherapy through an IV push was completed. Shortly
thereafter Daunorubicin would be administered and would drip
intravenously for about fifteen minutes. Once that was completed,
we were instructed that David would then have his first spinal tap.
For that he would be taken to another room where spinal taps
and bone marrow biopsies were performed. While he was being
wheeled down the hall, David entertained us through his wit and
jokes. He had an unusual display of calmness about him. My knees
were buckling as I walked alongside him on the gurney, but David
was all smiles and full of laughter. Dr. Gregory, who performed the
procedure, along with Susan, knew from that moment that there
was something unique about him. David's display of peace was

unparalleled. David's journey had begun, and those doctors and nurses were about to witness something very special.

> Consider it pure joy, my brothers and sisters, whenever you face trials of many kinds, because you know that the testing of your faith produces perseverance. Let perseverance finish its work so that you may be mature and complete, not lacking anything. (James 1:2–4)

David had asked not to have any anesthesia for that first spinal tap. (His first bone marrow biopsy performed just a few days earlier was accomplished under no anesthesia as well.) David had an extremely high pain tolerance—definitely not a family gene.

Spinal taps are performed when treating ALL for two reasons: 1) to check the spinal column for cancer cells and 2) to treat the central nervous system and brain by injecting chemotherapy directly into the spinal column. Chemotherapy administered into the bloodstream through an IV does not penetrate the central nervous system or brain, thus necessitating spinal taps. Regardless of whether cancer cells are detected in the spinal fluid, repeated spinal taps with chemotherapy injections would take place throughout the duration of treatment. One tiny cell that could go undiscovered had to be destroyed.

As David sat on the table, bending at the waist and leaning toward Susan, the oncologist began probing his back, looking for just the right spot to inject. David chuckled and joked throughout the whole procedure.

> Another shot of chemo ... Team Bring It goes strong.
> —David Mannino, May 16, 2011, Facebook post

By the time Dr. Gregory had completed the procedure, he too was offering up a joke or two. The mood was not strained or somber but rather light and joyful—hopeful. David made sure from that moment that the presence of joy and hope were prevalent at all times. There was no room for negative feelings no matter how difficult things might become.

At the completion of the procedure, Susan instructed David to lie down with the head of his bed tilted downward. That allowed the chemotherapy that was just injected into his spinal fluid to travel into his brain. He would have to remain that way, partially upside down, for an hour after each spinal tap. With every passing minute I felt like I was learning something new, and it was only intensifying. The thought of my son lying upside down so a toxic chemical could enter his brain was clearly unsettling. At that moment I realized that we were on a journey with so few options. Within two short weeks, we went from discussing graduation and preparation for college to cancer, ports, and chemotherapy treatments. Lord, where would this lead, and what were Your plans?

> Before I formed you in the womb I knew you. (Jeremiah 1:5)
>
> For you created my in most being; you knit me together in my mother's womb. (Psalm 139:13)
>
> Successful day one for Team Bring It! Chemo wasn't bad. Just doing what I know best … Bringing it!
> —David Mannino, May 16, 2011, Facebook post

David was wheeled back into his room. The first day of chemotherapy over! It was time to settle back and digest the previous two weeks, knowing that this journey would be long, but so thankful that God was walking alongside us. David could feel God's presence and gained strength through his Savior!

As the day progressed, many family members and friends stopped by David's room to offer their support. David's room was piled high with so many goodies, desserts, and bags of gifts that people had brought. Needless to say, his spirits as well as ours were uplifted by the outpouring of love by so many.

> Thanks for all of you who prayed for me today and who stopped by. Today is proof that the power of prayer and power of the Lord prevails! Team Bring It is ready to come full power tomorrow but still need everyone to continue tomorrow. Let's all have a great night and wake up strong tomorrow ready to bring it in whatever adversity presents itself.
> —David Mannino, May 17, 2011, Facebook post

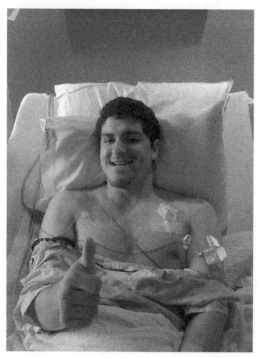

Day one of chemotherapy. David was ready to "Bring It."

Later that evening it was time for Tom and me to leave. It was my desire to stay overnight, but I knew I would be of better help to David if I went home and rested. I knew it would be a long two weeks. Driving home that night was so surreal. The thought kept racing through my mind that tomorrow would be his actual high school graduation and now David had a new assignment.

> The Lord makes firm the steps of the one who delights in Him. (Psalm 37:23)

How precious was life, and how precious was each day that God gave us! As we pulled into the driveway, exhausted, I got out of the car and proceeded to the mailbox instead of going directly indoors. As I began shuffling through the mail, a letter appeared. I recognized the writing. It was from David. With my heart fluttering and fingers trembling, I quickly tore it open. Where did this come from? As I opened it and started reading, tears welled up in my eyes. David had written me a thank-you letter. He was thanking me for all I had done for him over the past four years. As mothers, we sacrifice for our children and give immensely in hopes that we will make a difference in their lives. David recognized that and appreciated all that was done for him. There are no coincidences with God. At that moment, feeling overwhelmed and exhausted, God gave me a gift. His timing was perfect. David had apparently written and mailed that letter from school two weeks prior. But I received it on that first day—the day his treatment had started.

Wait for the Lord; be strong and take heart and
wait for the Lord! (Psalm 27:14)

Chapter 6

The next morning, I got up and immediately called David. Thank God for cell phones with a direct line. The days of waiting for an operator to connect your call were long over! I wanted to know how his night went and what he wanted me to bring him for breakfast. David was the most selective of my three children when it came to eating. I knew David's food preferences, and I felt that bringing him home-cooked meals was the least I could do for him. With every hospital admission, David never ate hospital food. Each hospital room was private and equipped with a small refrigerator. Needless to say, David's was filled with all of his favorites, with plenty to go around. For those first couple of weeks, room 5355 resembled a living room as much as a hospital room.

> Thanks everyone for bringing it today. Just one more down with many more to go. Special thanks to the Gerby family for stopping by tonight. The battle ensues tomorrow, so everyone continue to bring it at 100 percent and remember to never give up to adversity. And last but most importantly, remember to thank God!
>
> —David Mannino, May 17, 2011, Facebook post

Over the next couple of days, we all settled into our new routine. Tom would go to work in the morning as usual but then head over to the hospital after work to spend the evenings with David. I took a leave of absence from work so I could be with him throughout the entire day. I would prepare his meals in the morning and then bring them to the hospital. This would become our "new normal" when David had a hospital admission, which was every few weeks. Much of the treatment for ALL could be administered in the clinic as outpatient, but quite a bit required a hospital stay, especially when those blood transfusions were needed due to lowered blood levels. Suffice it to say that for the next several months we were at the hospital on a regular basis. The parking attendants were becoming all too familiar, as they frequently would open doors for me while I carried in bags of freshly cooked food.

We were ever so appreciative of all the loving friends and family who visited during those first few days to support David with so much love. He even received a special visitor, Mike Babcock, the head coach of the Detroit Red Wings. Since David was one of the shovelers for the Red Wings, he was fortunate enough to have the opportunity to get to know their coach. Mike was gracious enough to stop in and encourage David. He told David that the team was rooting for him. Usually it was David who would be cheering on the Detroit Red Wings, but ironically now it was the team pulling for David. David considered the Detroit Red Wings and coaching staff like his second family. He spent a tremendous amount of time down at the "Joe" (Joe Louis Arena) conversing, laughing, and getting to know the players well. Shoveling for them was truly the highlight of his high school years, so the visit by Mike Babcock was truly heartfelt and greatly appreciated. I was in the room, the morning that Mike stopped in. The first words out of his mouth were to me.

He said, "Mom, let me give you a hug."

Not only was he the coach of a major pro hockey team, but he was also a father. He knew that as a parent, it must have been grueling to watch my child in a hospital bed fighting cancer. He stayed for a little while as we chatted about his children and where they went to school and his love for Detroit. Then a Nigerian priest with a heavy accent came into the room. The priest did not recognize him and asked him if he worked at the hospital. Mike answered politely that no he did not work at the hospital but rather was just a friend of David's. How sweet and humble was his response? The priest then asked that all of us pray over David. Without reservation, Mike accepted the request, and the three of us prayed for David's healing. I will never forget that day and what it meant to David that the head coach of his beloved Red Wings came to visit him.

By that time, Andrea had returned from Israel and went directly to the hospital to see her brother. She had even decided to spend a couple of nights with him. David's room had a pullout cot of sorts, not exactly a bed but a close resemblance, so Andrea settled in. Andrea took on the role of a second mother to her brother. She wanted him to know how concerned she was and how much she loved him. Being away in Israel when she learned of the diagnosis was truly upsetting for her as she could not be at her brother's side. Therefore, she couldn't wait to get to the hospital to help comfort him, just like an older sister would do. She even brought David a T-shirt from Israel that was specially designed with the words "Team Bring It."

During those first few days, we also had the privilege of meeting many more nurses—caregivers who not only cared for David's medical needs but also cared for him emotionally. As crazy as this was, we started developing relationships with people we had never known before. We were quickly becoming "family." David developed a special bond with each one, especially with the nurses who worked the night shifts. David did not sleep very well during the night. While everyone else was sleeping, David was playing cards and chatting with the nurses. He was one of the older pediatric patients in the unit, and being so precocious and personable, he enjoyed their company. David learned early on to make the best of a challenging situation and to even have fun along the journey.

> Let's all have a strong day today and bring everything we have. Through God's power to have us bring it, we will have ability to defy odds and overcome adversity.
> —David Mannino, May 18, 2011, Facebook post

> Team Bring It is ready to roll 100 percent today! You want to say God doesn't exist? Well I'm proof He is and that He brings it all day every day 24-7!
> —David Mannino, May 19, 2011, Facebook post

Friday, May 20, was soon approaching, when another round of chemotherapy was scheduled. This time, it would not be administered through the port or spine but directly into his thighs. Susan, along with one other nurse, injected the chemotherapy simultaneously into his upper thighs and then repeated it. David didn't flinch. He took whatever was designed for him and praised God throughout it all.

> No discipline seems pleasant at the time, but painful. Later on, however, it produces a harvest of righteousness and peace for those who have been trained by it. (Hebrews 12:11)

Family supporting David during first hospital admission.

Chapter 7

With Team Bring It, you knock down doors and you kick down walls and anyone who tells you, you can't, you take your fears and your insecurities, and you roll them all up into a ball and you bring it. Let's *bring it* today at 100 percent and conquer the things that seem insurmountable with the grace from the Lord above. Never quit!

—David Mannino, May 21, 2011, Facebook post

Don't ask why and just say when all things in life don't make sense and that is why we are human and He is in control. All we can do is bring it in everything we do and believe that all has been planned for good! Team Bring It 24-7.

—David Mannino, May 22, 2011, Facebook post

David knew that God was in everything. He believed with unwavering faith that there was a clear and definite purpose behind his journey.

And we know that in all things God works for the good of those who love him, who have been called according to His purpose. (Romans 8:28)

David was adjusting to his new circumstances. That weekend he remained in the hospital without having to receive any chemotherapy. Steroids and other meds were given, but come Monday another spinal tap with chemotherapy would be administered.

> Battle begins tomorrow. With the Lord's power, nothing will stop me from bringing it!
> —David Mannino, May 22, 2011, Facebook post

> Knockout victory for Team Bring It! With the power of the Lord, nothing will stop us all from achieving greatness!
> —David Mannino, May 23, 2011, Facebook post

When the doctor and Susan walked into the room to administer that second spinal tap and chemotherapy injection, they suggested that from then on David be sedated with each spinal tap and bone marrow biopsy. This was not because of pain, necessarily, but rather to relax his muscles so there would be no tension in his body. Thus, Propofol was injected into his port, and within seconds David was asleep. I was in the room with David for each spinal tap and bone marrow biopsy. It was tough to watch my son fall asleep under anesthesia and observe the doctor as he penetrated his back with a needle. However, I knew that was the only way to conquer the enemy within. I would hold David's hands throughout all of the procedures and once they were completed, and the meds disconnected, that smiling face exuding peace and joy appeared again. David knew that in a few days he would be going home for the first time. That was where he placed his focus. However, his body was just starting to feel the effects of such potent drugs surging through his bloodstream.

The enemy is striking back hard, but I will
continue to bring it!
—David Mannino, May 23, 2011, Facebook post

Rough night but I'm still standing upright with
God. Team Bring It still rolls on!
—David Mannino, May 24, 2011, Facebook post

Chapter 8

When treating a cancer patient, it's not only the medical aspect (chemotherapy and other drugs) that is essential, but there is an emotional aspect that needs attention as well.

> New goal for Team Bring It—teach myself a new way to live.
> —David Mannino, May 24, 2011, Facebook post

The hospital insisted that David meet with Lisa, a social worker. She was a younger woman, very delightful, and very much interested in her patients. Lisa conversed with David for quite a while, assuring him that she was available to talk should he become discouraged or dismayed during this very long journey. She knew he was supposed to be celebrating his high school graduation and acceptance into a Big Ten University, but instead his future was on hold, with uncertainty looming. However, David's response to Lisa was quite different than what she expected. He wasn't angry or anxious or even jealous of his friends. David's joy was not dictated by circumstances but rather by knowing and having a personal relationship with Christ.

> "Not only so, but we also rejoice in our sufferings, because we know that suffering produces

perseverance; perseverance, character; and character, hope" (Romans 5:3-4). Getting stronger every day! Bringing it behind God's glory!
—David Mannino, May 25, 2011, Facebook post

David took that opportunity to share with Lisa that his strength came from the Lord. Lisa visited with him a few times during the seven months, each time offering her services. At one point during treatment she even discussed with me the possibility that maybe he was masking his anxiety because she couldn't understand how he could be at such peace. David never exhibited feelings of hostility, nor did he complain about having to fight the fury that was rampaging through his body. He simply surrendered to God's will. David would jokingly say to me, "Mom, they simply don't get it. I'm not depressed, and I'm not masking any ill feelings. I'm simply relying on God for strength."

> Fear not, for I am with you; be not dismayed, for I am your God; I will strengthen you, I will help you, I will uphold you with my righteous right hand. (Isaiah 41:10)

David was enveloped by the Holy Spirit and knew that God held him tight and was carrying him no matter what should come.

> I can do all things through Him who gives me strength. (Philippians 4:13)

Chapter *9*

Time to go home! First hospital admission was over! Home never felt so good like it did that day. While David was at the hospital, we rearranged his room so that he would be more comfortable, knowing that he would be spending quite a bit of time there. Tommy had just recently purchased a forty-six-inch flat screen TV for himself but instead set it up in his brother's room. He insisted that David deserved it more than him. Tommy struggled watching David fight this battle; giving him his brand-new TV wasn't even an issue. Video games are much more enjoyable on a large screen. David's room became his comfort zone. It was in that room where David laughed with friends, played video games, wrote papers for online college courses, vomited his guts out, attempted to sleep, and most importantly—connected with God!

> As you look at the photos of your life you wonder how you ever made it to where you are today. Take joy in friends, family, and God and take every moment for what it's worth and bring it 24–7. Never stop enjoying.
> —David Mannino, June 4, 2011, Facebook post

David and Tommy watching a hockey game
together on TV, at a family gathering.

It felt amazing to wake up and know that David was just across the
hall. Funny … he had been across the hall for the last seventeen
years, but now it was different. Something so normal and usual
became so special, a blessing. I took for granted what I assumed
would always exist. I was quickly learning how precious life really
was, and David was the instructor.

> When things are taken from you, you fight and
> gain them back. Team Bring It 24–7.
> —David Mannino, June 5, 2011, Facebook post

When David was discharged from the hospital, Susan had given
us multiple prescriptions to fill at the pharmacy, as David was to
take oral chemotherapy at home, along with other drugs. Susan
also gave us a calendar. That calendar was for only one month. It
became our guide and schedule for that month. With each new
month, a new calendar would be given. She wrote out what meds
were to be taken on which days and which days David would

have to return to the hospital or clinic for treatment. She also designated on the calendar which days David would have a spinal tap or bone marrow biopsy. There was a tremendous amount of traveling back and forth to the hospital, but our new routine was set in place for us. Life had changed now, and we had no input.

> Fourth round of chemotherapy today. With the power of God nothing will stand in my way from bringing it once again. It's a special thing to see God's work. You ought to get some seats to the show.
> —David Mannino, June 6, 2011, Facebook post

Chapter 10

Growing up, David greatly looked forward to June 7, his birthday. He loved all the festivities associated with it. Tom and I had often joked that for some reason, David's birthday seemed to last for a week. Maybe that was due to him being the baby of the family, but this year it would be different. After several rounds of chemotherapy and high doses of steroids, David woke up the morning of June 7 feeling awful. He was jittery from the steroids and nauseous from the chemotherapy. His whole body was under attack.

> Well not exactly how I envisioned my eighteenth
> birthday, but hey, that's life. Team Bring It, baby!
> —David Mannino, June 7, 2011, Facebook post

I was determined that, although cancer had altered our lives, it wasn't going to stop our celebration. David rested for most of the day, anticipating his family and friends coming over for dinner and birthday cake. He loved visiting with grandparents, aunts, uncles, cousins, and friends and was looking forward to that night. We gathered at the dining room table, and David desperately tried to enjoy himself. I had made his favorite meal, chicken parmesan with pasta, but it was evident on his face that the chemotherapy had taken its effects. Unfortunately, David was unable to eat anything.

He appreciated everyone that had come over and he attempted to make the best of the situation, but even opening up birthday gifts proved to be less enjoyable than usual. And the gigantic box of fireworks that Andrea had bought him did not generate the excitement he would have normally shown. Nothing replaces the gift of good health. However, David put a smile on his face and simply accepted what God had allowed into his life.

> For it has been granted to you on behalf of Christ not only to believe on Him, but also to suffer for Him. (Philippians 1:29)

Jeremy Camp, an admired Christian songwriter, released a powerful song in June 2003, entitled "I Still Believe." He wrote that song after the death of his first wife. One of the most heartfelt lines in the song states, "In brokenness I can see this is your will for me." David understood that, even though it didn't make sense to him or to me. He knew God had a reason for allowing this—an eternal purpose.

> In Him we were chosen having been predestined according to the plan of Him who works out everything in conformity with the purpose of His will. (Ephesians 1:11)

> Thanks to the millions and millions of my friends and family for the birthday wishes. Obviously, it's not what I had planned for my eighteenth birthday, but thanks to everyone, I'm gonna make it the best possible. Through all this, there is light, and through God I will obtain it. Until then let's make the most from each moment we all have and bring it!
> —David Mannino, June 7, 2011, Facebook post

For the next couple of days David did not receive any chemotherapy, allowing his blood counts to replenish. However, the steroids were still being administered, along with an antibiotic and other meds. David continued on course.

> Still standing. God is good! Refuse to lose.
> —David Mannino, June 10, 2011, Facebook post

> Make each moment worth a lifetime!
> —David Mannino, June 11, 2011, Facebook post

Chapter 11

David was drawing near the completion of the first stage—induction (inducing remission)—and on Monday, June 13, another spinal tap and bone marrow biopsy were scheduled. It was time to evaluate whether the cancer cells were eliminated in the bone marrow and continue to treat the spinal column. Even though there was never any visible presence of cancer cells in David's spinal column or brain, spinal taps were repeated throughout his entire journey. There were no exceptions to the protocol of treatment. From head to toe, David's body was being treated for ALL. It always amazed me how medical science, through a tremendous amount of testing and analyzing, was able to achieve the "perfect" protocol for not only this type of cancer but for others as well. Simply put, it reminded me of a recipe in a cookbook, a recipe that had to be followed without exception. Each day of each week was laid out like a roadmap.

> Gonna need everyone's prayers for tomorrow. Through God everything can be achieved! For tomorrow we go for remission!
> —David Mannino, June 12, 2011, Facebook post

Later on, that week we were thrilled to learn that David was on his way to remission. It sounded like the journey was half over, right? Actually not! David was responding positively to the chemotherapy, and remission was being induced, but there was so much ahead of him. The bone marrow biopsy evidenced that David still had 2 to 4 percent leukemic cells present. The doctors stated that they were looking for a 0 percent. There was well over one year of chemotherapy still in the future. However, our new goal was to achieve 0 percent within the next month. If 0 percent was not achieved by the end of July, then there would be reason for serious concern.

> Well, we're in remission, but the battle is far from over.
> —David Mannino, June 15, 2011, Facebook post

> Only do those things that please God. Otherwise what good are you doing to yourself or others? Love God and trust Him through all.
> —David Mannino, June 15, 2011, Facebook post

As the weeks were advancing and David was approaching the next stage, consolidation, he knew that the chemotherapy was only going to intensify. He dug deep into his faith and let God continue to steer the way. There was still so much uncertainty and so much treatment ahead, but David reconciled that God had already set the path in front of him and it was up to David to follow wherever the journey should lead. David continued to accept God's will and never allowed uncertainty to throw him into a spiritual decline.

> Unwavering faith!
> —David Mannino, June 16, 2011, Facebook post

> God is good. Now go out and find Him!
> —David Mannino, June 19, 2011, Facebook post

> Consolidation phase begins tomorrow. Through
> God all things can be achieved! Need everyone's
> prayers these next two months.
> —David Mannino, June 19, 2011, Facebook post

On June 20, 2011, the consolidation stage began with yet another spinal tap and methotrexate (chemotherapy) injection. Two other chemotherapy agents, Cytoxan and Cytarabine, were administered through IV, and the oral chemotherapy (Mercaptopurine) continued. For the remainder of that week, David received daily chemotherapy in one form or another.

> Follow God! He has and will continue to protect
> me and can do the same for you. You just gotta
> open yourself up to Him and feel His grace!
> —David Mannino, June 21, 2011, Facebook post

> God's got His Hands on me. Getting blasted yet
> feel normal. Can't say it enough of how good God
> is and how much each person Needs Him!
> —David Mannino, June 23, 2011, Facebook post

The following Monday, June 27, the intensity continued as another spinal tap was scheduled along with all the appropriate chemotherapy. Clearly stage 2 had started out fiercely, with no reprieve in sight. Even through those arduous treatments, David remained incredibly faithful. His demeanor continued to exhibit joy. He knew he was being tested but would not give in to doubt or disillusionment.

> Still going strong. God is good!
> —David Mannino, June 27, 2011, Facebook post

David received treatments throughout that week, and by June 30 his blood counts were so depleted from the chemotherapy obliterating them that Susan informed us of the necessity of a blood transfusion.

> Blood transfusion time.
> —David Mannino, June 30, 2011, Facebook post

"Dear Lord," I prayed, "please continue to put Your loving arms around my son." Watching David fight this battle and endure those oppressive drugs was the ultimate challenge for any parent. The only way we could help David was through prayer. There was nothing physically we could do for him. We were on a journey with other people making the decisions—directing every move.

> And yet God protects me again with today's roadblock, the blood transfusion. Bone marrow is getting blasted! Just taking each day with a smile, a hard hat, and faith!
> —David Mannino, June 30, 2011, Facebook post

> Yes, my soul, find rest in God; my hope comes from Him. Truly He is my rock and my salvation.
> (Psalm 62:5–6)

David was admitted back into the hospital for those series of first blood transfusions. What I had envisioned as one blood transfusion turned into many, which took place over several hours, with much waiting in between. First, they had to test and reconfirm his blood type. It would be catastrophic if the wrong type of blood was ever transfused into a patient. Once the blood type was confirmed, the blood was ordered. Once received, it was transfused through IV into his port, which took well over an hour. Upon completion of the transfusion, another blood draw would be in order to check blood counts. If the blood counts had not reached the desired levels then another transfusion would be given, and of course there was always the possibility of a reaction to the "new blood." It was a blessing that David never had a reaction, and we were very thankful for those anonymous donors who gave unselfishly of their blood, as David required six transfusions.

> Look good, feel good, God is good.
> —David Mannino, July 3, 2011, Facebook post

The journey was strenuous, painful, and long, but David as well as our family clearly felt the strength of God. For all that was required, David continued to accept it without complaint and traversed through.

David was released from the hospital in time to celebrate the Fourth of July. However, he needed to stay on schedule because the following morning we traveled back to the hospital for another spinal tap, along with the chemotherapy treatments.

> Even after six transfusions, still standing strong. God is good.
> —David Mannino, July 6, 2011, Facebook post

> "What happens when God breathes your way? Every enemy will be defeated, obstacles will be overcome, favor will increase, dreams will come to pass."
> —David Mannino, July 8, 2011, Facebook post

Chapter *12*

As we approached the middle of July, now two months into treatment, the hospital was feeling like a second home. David was developing relationships with the oncology nurses as well as with the other patients and their parents. David became the big brother to all. A beautiful ten-year-old little girl who was battling bone cancer, and who needed to have a leg amputated, turned to David for support. Her mother shared with me that David strengthened her emotionally, sharing his faith and giving her reasons as to why she should be happy even though she was going through a difficult time in her very young life. She also shared that David would help her daughter pass the time by doing arts and crafts with her, something she loved. This was a difficult journey for anybody to go through, especially for those children whose lives were altered at such a young age. Truly only those who have gone through it thoroughly understand it.

One morning as I stepped off the elevator on the fifth floor, heading toward David's room, I was met by a nurse who shared with me how different David was from her other patients. She also shared with me that the other nurses would try to get David as their patient whenever there was a shift change. David had a way of not only making them laugh but also uplifting them and encouraging them to persevere no matter what life would throw at them. A positive attitude was one thing, but it was his charismatic magnetism that they admired most. For some reason, these nurses felt like they could trust David, sharing with him things about their personal lives. During one hospital admission, it was approaching 11:00 p.m., time for Tom and me to leave the hospital for that evening. As we were saying good night to David, one of his nurses walked into his room and asked him if he could help her with her chemistry. Apparently, she was preparing for her master's degree and was struggling with chemistry. David had just finished all honors classes and was extremely proficient in chemistry and physics. He responded that he would be happy to help her whenever she was able to take her break. Her break would come after midnight. Since sleeping was difficult for David, due to the side effects of the chemotherapy and drugs, the late timing was no problem. He would have rather been productive than struggle to fall asleep in his hospital bed.

> Even with a miserable start to the day, God gives me a great evening.
> —David Mannino, July 12, 2011, Facebook post

David also developed special relationships with all of the oncologists who treated him, especially Dr. Scott. Dr. Scott was not only a great pediatric oncologist, but he was like a grandfather to all of his young patients, with whom he cultivated many special relationships. David was no exception. He recognized that David wasn't the average patient. The relationship between David and Dr. Scott was an intellectual relationship of sorts. He knew David was intending to go to medical school and that David's efforts in researching information on ALL was his greatest ally in the fight. David understood the journey better than most and required realistic answers to his myriad of questions. Not only did David and Dr. Scott discuss every facet of ALL, but they were also both sports enthusiasts, rooting for the same teams, namely the University of

Michigan Wolverines and the Detroit Red Wings. David and Dr. Scott would strategize plays and discuss which players should be traded. They genuinely forged a unique bond. It was almost as if Dr. Scott could see himself in David, when he was David's age.

One morning when Dr. Scott appeared on the oncology floor to examine his patients, he arrived at David's room, but David was not there. Dr. Scott jokingly explained to me that he looked all over his room and the adjoining areas, but David was nowhere to be found. He thought, *Where could this kid be with an IV pole attached to him?* Upon entering the nurse's station, he discovered that David was sitting in a chair with several nurses surrounding him, joking, laughing, and socializing.

Dr. Scott exclaimed, "Oh there he is! He reminds me of Jesus and the disciples." As strange as it was, David really embraced every moment, and his inexplicable joy radiated at all times, becoming someone who was greatly admired.

> Rejoice in the Lord always. I will say it again: Rejoice! ... And the peace of God, which transcends all understanding, will guard your hearts and your minds in Christ Jesus. (Philippians 4:4, 7)

With their love of sports, Dr. Scott and David both agreed that they would attend a Michigan game together once the season resumed. David had a friend who was the executive secretary to the athletic director. She was able to arrange for David and Dr. Scott to watch a game from the press box. I don't think I had ever seen David so excited about a sporting event than for that game. Unfortunately, due to David's compromised health condition, they had to cancel. David was extremely disappointed, but Dr. Scott assured him that they would reschedule once he completed treatment. He even gave David a framed picture of the Michigan Stadium—"the Big House." David hung it on his wall at the entrance of his bedroom, where it still hangs today. In fact, when David was first diagnosed, the newly acquired football coach for the Michigan Wolverines sent him a letter expressing his sadness in learning that David, an upcoming freshman, had been diagnosed with a threatening cancer. David's gratitude for the letter is reflected in his own letter that follows.

May 27, 2011

Hello, Coach,

This is David Mannino.

First off let me say how humbled and honored I was to receive your letter in the mail today. The last couple of days have been really hard on me adjusting to life with cancer right at the end of my senior year, and your thoughts and prayers brought tears to my eyes and really brightened me up. Ever since I was a child, the University of Michigan has been a home for me. I visit Ann Arbor numerous times throughout the year and religiously watch every football game till the final whistle blows. I just graduated from U of D Jesuit at the top of my class and was supposed to attend the University of Michigan in the fall, but obviously because of the complications of the sickness, that must be put on a temporary hold. I do not know how much you may know about my situation, but I was recently diagnosed with an aggressive cancer (ALL) that has really changed things in my life drastically. ALL is a type of lymphoma/leukemia that involves the replicated T-cells in the body, and it involves about a year and a half of treatment, approximately nine months of which are intensive chemotherapy. If things go according to treatment, which they are thus far, I should be put into remission by the middle of June and be able to live a normal life in society by the end of February or early March. By the power of God, despite the sorrow of the situation, I can see God's hands throughout the entire process. I have already seen a rapid reduction in the number of cancer cells, which truly attests to the power of prayer and the Lord. It is very easy to lose faith and seem angry throughout this whole process, but I can honestly say that my faith has become even stronger as I see many individuals who once were not firmly rooted in Christ take on a greater relationship with Him through my situation. The feeling that God is using me to further His kingdom and further His plan really proves to me that I will get through this and conquer whatever evils are coming my way! In my off time of school, I play AAA hockey for Little Caesars, and actually one of my best friend's mom works with your boss in the athletic office. I actually talked to her today about your letter, and we both talked about the great character you have for taking time out of your day to reach me. In addition to my love for Michigan football, I also love the Detroit Red Wings, and for the last two years I have worked for the Wings as a member of their ice crew. Like I said before, Michigan football is my ultimate love, and no matter win or lose, the Wolverines have an irreplaceable spot in my heart. When I conquer this enemy one day, I would love to volunteer my time to the team that has given me so much in my life, in whatever way that I can. It would be my dream to touch the M Go Blue banner as a cancer survivor and feel the pulse of the hundreds of thousands of fans rumble the Wolverine name throughout the Big House. If there is anything I can do for the team in any way in terms of motivation or anything, please don't hesitate to ask. This upcoming season means more to me than any other season in the past, and I'm really looking forward to your great future as new head coach. Please tell the boys on the team how much they mean to me! I love Michigan football!

There's simply nothing else like it. Tell them to bring it in every battle or war they have, just like I am every day with my enemy!

Thanks for everything and *go Blue*

David Mannino

David #22 centers the U of D Jesuit seniors from the shores of Belle Isle. In the distance the GM building towers over the Detroit River as the Ambassador Bridge connects Canada and USA.

David skating for the Little Caesars Hockey Team

The ultimate faceoff, David #22

Chapter *13*

July 14, 2011, was the day David met with another pediatric oncologist. We felt it was in David's best interest to get a second opinion on the fact that David had not reached 0 percent in the previous bone marrow biopsy. Possibly another professional opinion could shed additional information. David and that doctor connected immediately. We discovered that David had gone to high school with his sons. Funny how life intertwines people together. He too agreed that after the conclusion of that first stage, David should have had no cancer cells present in the previous biopsy. However, he felt hopeful that he would achieve a zero at the next biopsy, which was scheduled for July 18. If cancer cells were still present, additional medical intervention would have to be considered, namely a bone marrow transplant. Just the words *bone marrow transplant* sent a shock through my body, and I only felt worse as the doctor continued to explain the bone marrow transplant process. He stated that the chemotherapy that would be required to prepare the body for transplant was even more intense than what David was already receiving. He compared it to a field of lush grass. The chemotherapy that was presently being administered would be equivalent to patches of dirt on that lush grass, while the chemotherapy administered for transplant would eradicate all the grass, leaving only dirt. The entire system would be suppressed, allowing the transplanted blood to be received and engrafted. Are you kidding me! I was feeling distressed with that news! I couldn't even imagine more potent chemotherapy than what he was already receiving. I had had enough of this disease. David, however, remained fearless. He continued to set the tone for fighting this monster.

> Don't believe in the report of misery but the Lord's report of grace.
> —David Mannino, July 16, 2011, Facebook post

The doctor had instructed us to stay on course and agreed with our present doctors. He indicated that the next bone marrow biopsy would dictate whether a transplant should be considered. He also recommended that Tom, Tommy, Andrea, and I get tested to see if any of us matched David as a prospective donor. As it turned out, Andrea was a perfect match. God had stepped in and allowed us to have that gift, which gave us peace of mind, knowing that should David need a transplant, his sister would be the donor.

> So do not fear, for I am with you; do not be dismayed, for I am your God. I will strengthen you and help you; I will uphold you with my righteous right Hand. (Isaiah 41:10)

Once again, we were playing the waiting game. In a couple of days, we would know whether this all-consuming and agonizing journey would only get worse. In the meantime, David was dealing with ongoing nausea that made it difficult to keep food down and precipitated into a GI dilemma. His doctors were uncertain as to what was causing this, and they could not stop it. After a couple of weeks with no resolve, they suggested that David have an EGD (esophagogastroduodenoscopy). This involved inserting a scope down his throat and into the esophagus, stomach, and duodenum. By 4:00 p.m. that afternoon, David was wheeled into the procedure room. Propofol was administered, and Dr. Anthony, the GI physician, performed the EGD. We learned that David was suffering from a chemotherapy -induced ulcer. Dr. Anthony explained that any food or liquid, including saliva, which came in contact with the ulcer gave David the nauseous feeling that caused him to spit or vomit. Therefore, he was placed on medication to help heal the ulcer, which took a few weeks. Because of that unexpected complication, David's chemotherapy schedule was pushed back one week to allow the ulcer to begin healing. However, the bone marrow biopsy remained.

> Bone marrow biopsy tomorrow. Need everyone's prayers for a zero!
> —David Mannino, July 17, 2011, Facebook post

Just when you think you can't handle anymore, God comes in to rescue you, to pick you up, and carry you through.

> Zero … Thanks to the Lord.
> —David Mannino, July 20, 2011, Facebook post

What a relief! Praise God! At that point, no transplant was needed! One major hurdle was behind us. We all joked about that being the first zero David had ever received on a test, and believe me, we were thrilled. The thought that we had escaped the possibility of having to have a bone marrow transplant was incredibly gratifying. God had given us a powerful gift of grace.

> Walking behind God restores.
> —David Mannino, July 24, 2011, Facebook post

One week off of chemotherapy felt like a lifetime. It gave David a chance to come up for air, ever so briefly. By the following week another spinal tap was scheduled, along with a number of other chemotherapy treatments. In a few more weeks, David would enter the third stage. I felt is if we were traversing through an obstacle course, checking off each event that David completed, aiming toward the finish line.

> Revitalized.
> —David Mannino, July 30, 2011, Facebook post

> Satisfied? … Find God!
> —David Mannino, July 31, 2011, Facebook post

Chapter *14*

Summer was well underway, and although our original plans for that summer never came to pass, spending time together as a family, whether at home or the hospital, was of the utmost importance. The whole experience taught us much, and although I would never have chosen this journey, God taught us the real meaning of what life should be about. Tomorrow is never a guarantee, and truthfully, each day that we are given should be cherished and lived with great purpose.

While David and I were taking a brief walk one afternoon, he and I were engaging in a lighthearted conversation when he blurted out, "Mom, nobody wants cancer, but I'd do it all over again to become the man I've become."

Although I knew what he meant, I almost couldn't comprehend what he was saying. David was already a person of good character. He was loving, giving, and considerate of others, but that's not what he was referring to at all. He was referring to living for Christ and trusting in Him throughout all uncertainty. David would always remind me that life was really a dress rehearsal preparing us for the final act.

> When you have looked the devil in the eyes in the midst of a seemingly insurmountable battle and are able to laugh at and deflect his futile attempts to alter your faith in God, understand that His Grace is at your fingertips and that you're almost there in achieving victory. Team Bring It!
>
> —David Mannino,
> August 16, 2011, Facebook post

It was at that moment in this journey that I knew David had experienced a relationship, a oneness with God like never before. There was an emotional and spiritual transformation that had taken place. His courage and his strength were so deep and profound. The enemy that David was fighting would not be allowed to tear down his foundation but rather be used as the means to become stronger to fulfill God's purposes.

> And let us run with perseverance the race marked out for us, fixing our eyes on Jesus, the pioneer and perfecter of faith. (Hebrews 12:1–2)
>
> In the book of Genesis, Joseph addresses his brothers, who sold him into slavery: "Don't be afraid. Am I in the place of God? You intended to harm me, but God intended it for good to accomplish what is now being done, the saving of many lives" (Genesis 50:19–20)

David knew that God was at work in his life through all the pain and suffering. Cancer intends to destroy, but when God is at work, greater things, things that cannot be measured with human hands, become evident. David did not argue with God but rather accepted the challenge, the assignment, and believed wholeheartedly that God's will would ultimately prevail.

> For I consider the sufferings of this present time
> are not worthy to be compared with the glory that
> is to be revealed to us. (Romans 8:18)

Chapter *15*

By mid-August, the doctors informed us that it was time for David to have a PET scan. A PET scan is an imaging test that resembles an MRI. A radioactive substance is administered to help identify any disease in the body, and it is frequently used when assessing whether treatment is working on cancer patients. August 18 was the day of David's PET scan. Both Andrea and I sat with David in a small room in the nuclear medicine area of the hospital as we waited for him to be injected with the radioactive tracer. Once it was administered, David had to wait approximately one hour for it to be absorbed throughout his body. Then he was moved to the imaging room and placed on a table that glided into a tubular-shaped machine. Andrea and I were able to watch this from a small window in the door of the x-ray room. I could see the table moving through the tube with what appeared to be a beam of blue light marking off sections of his body from head to toe. David was as still as could be. No movement was allowed so as not to skew the testing. All I could do was pray that no cancer cells would be evidenced. *Please, Lord,* I thought, *watch over my son, and please allow this PET scan to be negative.* One day later, we were given great news.

> Negative PET scan. Glory to God!
>
> —David Mannino,
> August 19, 2011, Facebook post

Over the next three days, David had another bone marrow biopsy and spinal tap. It was our prayer that those would be negative as well.

> Bone marrow and PET scan are negative! Power of prayer. Four more months of intense chemo. Still need prayers.
> —David Mannino,
> August 23, 2011, Facebook post

David had a few days where the chemotherapy schedule lightened, allowing his body to regain some strength. Stage 3—interim maintenance—was only days away, and the intensity would then increase.

> Feel great. Must mean it's time to get chopped back down.
> —David Mannino,
> August 26, 2011, Facebook post

> "Like stars across the sky we were born to shine!"— Andrea Bocelli

> Phase 3 starts today. Glory to God! Need everyone's prayers this week.
> —David Mannino,
> August 29, 2011, Facebook post

Chapter *16*

Stage 3 was unlike the other stages in that the chemotherapy treatments were administered in a very set and unique manner. David would be admitted into the hospital on a Monday, where a very high dose of chemotherapy, methotrexate, would drip through an IV into his port for twenty-four hours. That chemotherapy was so toxic that after the twenty-four hours, David would receive another drug called Leucovorin to flush out the methotrexate and neutralize its harmful side effects. Leucovorin would help protect healthy cells from the chemotherapy and would be administered multiple times until the levels of methotrexate would dissipate to a negligible amount. This was measured through repeated blood tests, and that process would take anywhere from five to seven days. David would have to remain in the hospital the entire time. This routine would take place every other week for eight weeks. And, if that wasn't enough, there were still other chemotherapy agents being administered and the perpetual spinal taps and bone marrow biopsies performed.

> Spinal taps and methotrexate ... To good health.
> —David Mannino,
> September 2, 2011, Facebook post

I had never seen a bag of chemotherapy like the methotrexate. Not only was it enormous, two liters in size, but it was bright yellow, resembling a two-liter bottle of Mountain Dew. Just the thought of a two-liter bag filled with toxins slowly dripping into my child was discomforting. I could see on the nurses' faces a real sense of empathy when they had to administer that chemotherapy. We were clearly in the thick of it now with still much more to come.

> Sometimes you have to go through the fire to achieve the pearl.
> —David Mannino,
> September 5, 2011, Facebook post

David's spirits remained upbeat and positive. Thank God he was able to make the best of every situation.

> Gotta love jamming to Michael Jackson and Jack Johnson in the halls of the peds floor. Glory to God.
> —David Mannino,
> September 5, 2011, Facebook post

David was in the hospital for that first round of methotrexate for one full week, greatly anticipating his discharge.

> I am coming home! Thanks be to God.
> —David Mannino,
> September 5, 2011, Facebook post

Chapter 17

Four months into this journey, other than a few strands that had fallen out, David was still sporting a mop of hair on his head. Susan stated how unusual that was and insisted that soon his hair would fall out. All patients that far along in treatment have no hair, but David's beautiful, thick, curly brown hair was holding on strong. In fact, with much anticipation of his hair falling out, David insisted that we let it go and not cut it at all. He wouldn't even trim it. Instead of losing all of his hair, it continued to grow and became bushy. I guess he reasoned that instead of cutting it, he'd just wait for it to all fall out. That day never happened! As treatment continued, it thinned out a small amount, but he never lost it all, nor did it look patchy. Truly, God was in control! I continuously suggested to David that cutting his hair or at least trimming it would take on a cleaner look, as characteristically, his hair never grew long. It just grew up and out, but David insisted that his hair and beard, for that matter, remain untouched. Well ... at least until Lexi came along.

A few months before David was diagnosed, he met a lovely girl from New Jersey. Lexi was also admitted to the University of Michigan and was an upcoming freshman like David. For several months they got to know each other over the phone as they shared their dreams and goals for their bright futures. Two young adults, miles away from each other, coming from similar backgrounds, with birthdays just one day apart, had forged a friendship that would never be forgotten. Lexi was still in New Jersey but would be leaving for Michigan to begin her college education. Not only was she beautiful and intelligent but also compassionate, characteristics David loved. He had shared the news of his diagnosis with her and the necessity to defer his enrollment into the University of Michigan for a later date. As shocking as that news was, she and David continued their friendship. She became the radiant star in his life. Soon she would be in Michigan, and David waited to see her with much anticipation. The day before his first visit to Ann Arbor to see Lexi, the clippers came out. It was time to cut the hair. All of a sudden, the anxiety of whether or not to cut his hair didn't matter. Looking well-trimmed and handsome took priority. One of David's best friend's stepfather, Bryce, took it upon himself to handle the task. Bryce not only cut David's hair but also got the beard under control as well. Needless to say, the end product was a success, and David, looking very GQ, was ready for his date. Getting together with Lexi brought so much joy and normalcy into David's life, even if it was only temporary.

They continued to talk often, and David made the trip to Ann Arbor only a few times, as his health permitted. David's plan was to get through those first nine months of intense chemotherapy and then begin at the University of Michigan during the spring term. David's doctors even suggested that he finish the last year of maintenance chemotherapy at the University of Michigan Hospital. We all agreed with the doctors and the plan was set.

Chapter 18

Today's the day! Not yesterday, nor tomorrow, and certainly not two weeks from now to discover the promises that you have and will receive from God. It might look like your trouble will never come to pass, yet all you have to do is believe and have the faith that He is in control and that you will receive His grace when you meditate on His promises. Just like Jesus was killed and buried on a Friday and then raised again on a Sunday, you too shall receive your Sunday through faith.

—David Mannino,
September 12, 2011, Facebook post

David was home for about two weeks in between the first and second round of methotrexate. His blood counts had lowered quite a bit from the first round, so his doctors gave him a couple of additional days for his blood to replenish before continuing. However, his regimen of daily oral chemotherapy remained.

"Even though I walk through the valley of the shadow of death, I will fear no evil, for you are with me; your rod and your staff, they comfort me" (Psalm 23:4). You may be in a valley of death, but this promise says walk through, not stuck in or live in for eternity. This is a promise that gives confirmation that this valley shall pass when we are with God. It might be a journey but we will all walk through it, and that's a promise from the only one who is certain to keep promises! Team Bring It!

—David Mannino,
September 14, 2011, Facebook post

David was passing me on the staircase coming down from his bedroom when he shared with me how he was passing through a valley. He exclaimed that he was clinging to the promises of God, and God clearly states that we are never stuck but simply journeying through the valley. The valley he was traveling through would not last forever. What strength and confidence he displayed, and once again David was my teacher.

Chapter 19

One morning as I was preparing breakfast in the kitchen and David was in his bedroom, the phone rang. It was a gentleman who worked at the hospital. He stated that there was going to be an article written in the newspaper covering the topic of cancer and teens. He went on to explain that he had contacted the pediatric oncology unit and asked for potential patients to be interviewed. David was selected. Before he would give David's name and number to the reporter, he wanted his permission. Without hesitation David agreed. Within a few hours the reporter, who was a medical reporter from the *Detroit Free Press*, called our house inquiring of David. She and I chatted for a while on the phone as I explained to her that if she was looking for a doom-and-gloom teenager battling cancer, she had the wrong one. She went on to explain that her only purpose behind the article was to write a documentation of how teenagers cope with fighting cancer. *Great*, I thought! I knew it would be an intriguing conversation. She went on to say that since David's chemotherapy schedule was so demanding, along with her work schedule, it would be best if she just called him on his cell and interviewed him over the phone. After all, David was eighteen and did not need my approval or written authorization. With that, I gave her David's cell phone number, and within a day or two she contacted him. The day she called, David was walking upstairs to go into his room. When I discovered it was her on the phone, I naturally followed behind him, but I respected David's privacy as he entered his room and shut the door. Well, I respected his privacy only as much as I could hear with my ear to his door. Perfect! He had the phone on speaker. An intriguing conversation it was. David shared his Christian principles with her and expressed that having cancer was obviously no fun, but through God, family, and friends, you get through it. David explained that he actually received strength through encouraging others. I will never forget the close of that conversation. The reporter told David how much she enjoyed the interview and asked if she could call him again sometime in the future. She stated that she felt like she needed to talk to him again, not about cancer but about life in general.

David's answer was simple: "Absolutely. In fact, why don't you become my friend on Facebook?"

David's ability to inspire people, even strangers was remarkable. The conversation ended and David stepped out of his room. "Mom," he said, "why didn't you just open the door and come in!"

Chapter 20

Although David was feeling pretty beat up from all the treatment, Andrea's birthday was in a couple of days, and he wanted to celebrate with her. As much as he didn't feel like leaving the house, he agreed to a family dinner out. I thought that going out would allow him to have a change of environment, other than the routine of our house or the hospital. But quite honestly David would rather have been home, as he was feeling so crummy. He put on a happy face, but his eyes told the real story. There was nothing I could do for him to make him feel better. I so desperately wanted to take this from him. I so desperately wanted him to feel healthy and strong again, but David had the right attitude. He simply kept his eyes on his faith, not his illness, and remained a testimony to all.

> No matter what dream you may have in your heart, through God it will come to pass when you are in accordance to Him and you believe. Never give up hoping, dreaming, or believing because your day is coming.
>
> —David Mannino,
> September 17, 2011, Facebook post

David and Andrea touring Rome, Italy 2009

Well, back to the hospital. Time to bring it once
again!

—David Mannino,
September 19, 2011, Facebook post

On Monday, September 19, David returned to the hospital to
continue with the methotrexate. This time, however, there
was an unexpected setback. It took an additional week for the
methotrexate to diminish from David's system. During that two-
week battle, David's spirits were remarkable. He remained positive
anticipating his release. However, with each passing day and the
testing of his blood, it became quite evident that this would have
to take its course. Meanwhile we were praying that no additional
complications would set in.

> Ephesians 6:10–17: "Finally, be strong in the Lord
> and in his mighty power. Put on the full armor
> of God, so that you can take your stand against

the devil's schemes. For our struggle is not against flesh and blood, but against the rulers, against the authorities, against the powers of this dark world and against the spiritual forces of evil in the heavenly realms. Therefore put on the full armor of God, so that when the day of evil comes, you may be able to stand your ground, and after you have done everything, to stand. Stand firm then, with the belt of truth buckled around your waist, with the breastplate of righteousness in place, and with your feet fitted with the readiness that comes from the gospel of peace. In addition to all this, take up the shield of faith, with which you can extinguish all the flaming arrows of the evil one. Take the helmet of salvation and the sword of the Spirit, which is the word of God."

—David Mannino,
September 28, 2011, Facebook post

Just before David went into the hospital for that second round of methotrexate, a family friend had invited us to a Detroit Tigers game in a private suite. Originally David was to be released in time to attend, but with that setback, it was questionable. David was a huge Detroit Tigers fan and watched every game on TV, so to have an opportunity to cheer for them in a private suite was something he genuinely looked forward to. The fact that Lexi was planning on attending with him made it even more exciting. As it turned out, however, David was not discharged in time for the game. David's love for sports was such an enormous diversion for him. It gave him an opportunity to focus on something else besides cancer and how his life had been so radically interrupted. Once again, he would have to rely on watching the game on TV. Needless to say, David was extremely disappointed, but he accepted the circumstances without complaint. He knew from the onset of this

to be David. What could have happened? I answered frantically, asking him if he was okay.

"I am great, Mom," he answered. He continued, "Do you know why I wasn't able to go home tonight?"

What was he talking about! Of course I knew why he wasn't released. He still had traces of the methotrexate in his blood.

When I responded with that answer, David simply said, "No, Mom, that's not why. After you and Dad left, one of the night nurses came into my room and we got talking. I had the opportunity to give a testimony of my faith and share the importance of a personal relationship with Christ."

He went on to tell me that it was an awesome conversation and that she had never thought about her faith in such a way. Needless to say, I sat up in bed in complete amazement. God was working before my eyes. That night at the hospital, I did not tell David that God had spoken to me. God had whispered ever so quietly to me that that was the reason for the delayed discharge.

"Good night, Mom!" David said. "See you tomorrow! I'm coming home."

> Finnnnnnallllllyyyyyyy after two long weeks I'm
> coming ... home! Thanks be to God!
> —David Mannino,
> October 1, 2011, Facebook post

It's interesting, how the simple things in life are really the most important. Having David home after two grueling weeks was more wonderful than anything else life could offer, even if it was only for one week! Round three was approaching quickly.

Philippians 1:19–20: "For I know that this will turn out for my deliverance through your prayer and the supply of the spirit of Jesus Christ, according to my earnest expectation and hope that is nothing I shall be ashamed, but with all boldness, as always, so now also Christ will be magnified in my body, whether by life or by death."

—David Mannino,
October 2, 2011, Facebook post

Chapter 21

Fall was upon us! The Detroit Tigers were in the playoffs. The Detroit Lions had just begun their season, along with college football, and the Detroit Red Wings were back at the Joe! David was loving every minute following his favorite teams.

Tigers game.

—David Mannino,
October 3, 2011, Facebook post

Although David had been home only two days from the hospital and was feeling a little tired, the Detroit Tigers were playing the New York Yankees at Comerica Park in game three of the playoffs, and David's favorite pitcher was pitching. Oh, how he wanted to go to that game. With the aid of Craigslist and a little perseverance, Tom surprised David with two tickets. As thrilled as I was that David was going to the game, I was also concerned about his physical well-being. He was weak, and he had a very compromised immune system. With so many people in a huge stadium, there was reason for concern. David's doctors approved him to go but encouraged him to be extra careful when coming into contact with other people. That night when Tom and David got home from Comerica Park, I was anxious to hear all the details. The Tigers took the win, so it must've been a great night.

David walked in the door with a glow on his face, but the details he gave me were far from what I expected. David did exclaim that the Tigers played outstanding, and it was an awesome night, but that was all he said about the game. He continued by telling me about a conversation he had with a man he had never met before. It was a man who, when he left for the game that night, had no idea he would be meeting a boy who would influence his life forever. That man sat next to David. Idle conversation turned into a life-changing exchange. David shared with that man his cancer diagnosis and more importantly, his faith. He told him how God had transformed his life in spite of the cancer and that real strength and courage come from God alone. When David took his baseball cap off, the man thought he looked familiar. David mentioned that he was a shoveler for the Detroit Red Wings. The man attended Red Wings games regularly and recognized a familiar face. That three-hour baseball game made a huge impact on both David and that gentleman. However, it wasn't baseball that bonded them together, nor was it baseball that occupied the majority of their conversation. It was David's testimony of faith that was the game-changer. A few years ago, I received a letter from that man, whose name I learned was Craig.

In Craig's own words, "I still wonder why I was so lucky to have met David that night. Why did he have such an impact on my life? What brought us together among thousands of people in seats next to one another? What reason did we begin talking, for no reason, only to leave feeling like I had known him forever but really only a few hours … Two strangers meet at a baseball game in October, the young man touches the life of the other in ways that really cannot be explained other than the young man was meant for greater things and was meant to touch lives in ways that many can never explain. Two strangers left as strangers no more after only a few hours, at least for this one. I left with what I feel is a friend for life."

There are no coincidences with God, who continuously intertwines circumstances and lives together. Not only was David an inspiration and blessing to Craig that night, but Craig also positively influenced David and Craig has continued to uplift the Mannino family.

> The NBA has a slogan during the playoffs, "Where amazing happens," but I'm sorry to say that the amazing happens when you're following God's word and living according to His will. Then and only then do amazing things actually happen because it's during that time when you receive God's favor.
>
> —David Mannino,
> October 4, 2011, Facebook post

> 1 Timothy 6:11–12: "But you, as a man of God, flee from these things; and pursue righteousness, godliness, faithfulness, love, steadfastness, gentleness. Fight the good fight of the faith, take hold of the eternal life to which you were called when you testified so well to your faith before many witnesses." The epitome of Team Bring It!
>
> —David Mannino,
> October 5, 2011, Facebook post

Chapter 22

David was mentally preparing for round three of the methotrexate, scheduled for the following week. Before that day, however, he continued monitoring the Detroit Tigers, anticipating many victories.

> Now that's bringing it. Do I hear three home runs?
> —David Mannino,
> October 6, 2011, Facebook post

> Already bringing in the relief pitcher ... Yankee fans, it's time to worry.
> —David Mannino,
> October 6, 2011, Facebook post

> 1 Corinthians 9:24: "Do you not know that those who run in a race all run, but only one receives the prize? Run in such a way that you may win." Tonight the Tigers brought it, ran in the race, and ran in the race to win!
> —David Mannino,
> October 6, 2011, Facebook post

By the end of that week David was starting to feel stronger since he was in between rounds of the chemotherapy. He was feeling well enough to think about heading back to Joe Louis Arena, otherwise known as the Joe, the home of the Red Wings.

> Bringing the boots down from retirement ... Because if I'm not mistaken, I'm feeling pretty good. Not in the hospital until Monday, and I heard there's a Wings game tonight.
> —David Mannino,
> October 7, 2011, Facebook post

David was referring to hockey skates. He was itching to get back on the ice and shovel for the Red Wings, but he settled for watching a game from behind the net, next to the Zamboni door, his usual spot, along with all the other shovelers.

> After six longgggg months (and still with two more to come), finalllllly going back to the Joe!
> —David Mannino,
> October 7, 2011, Facebook post

> Great night. Can't wait till January, when I can return for good, but it was a good taste for the future. Want to give a shout out to all my family down at the Joe, players, and staff everyone ... And of course, a special shout out to DMills 20, my favorite Wing on the roster. Thank the Lord for giving me a great night with many more to come!
> —David Mannino,
> October 8, 2011, Facebook post

We were so thrilled that David had a great weekend with his favorite pastime, especially since Monday was coming quickly.

> Need prayers for tomorrow. Back to the fight.
> —David Mannino,
> October 9, 2011, Facebook post

We arrived at the hospital as scheduled, and within an hour round three of the methotrexate was initiated. Three days prior, David was feeling as normal as possible and was at the Joe trying to live life as usual, but *this* day, the reality of his situation was ever so present.

> Walking back into the fire but through the Lord I will crawl back into the light and prevail. Thanks everyone for all your prayers, continue them please, it's fighting time!
> —David Mannino,
> October 10, 2011, Facebook post

That third round of methotrexate went much better than the previous round. There were no complications or unwanted events. The only notable event that week was David's interview by a local TV news reporter for a promotional ad for the movie *Puss in Boots* (released October 2011). I, however, had missed all the excitement. One afternoon, a local reporter came to the hospital to interview a patient. I had just left the hospital to go home and make David's dinner. By the time I got back, the interview was over. We were never informed that this was going to take place or that David would be interviewed. Apparently, one of our local news stations had made previous arrangements with the hospital, and the reporter, along with *Puss in Boots*, arrived on the fifth floor and asked the nurses which patient they would recommend for her to interview. Which patient would be able to carry on an impromptu conversation? David was selected. I was so disappointed that I wasn't there to witness the conversation, but just by looking at the picture taken, it was evident that David and the reporter connected. David had everyone laughing: nurses, patients, and the reporter herself. He wasn't shy when the cameras started rolling. In fact, David was all about making sure that the other patients were entertained. It was very heart-wrenching for him to watch those young kids, mostly ten years of age and younger, fighting cancer. Even though David was fighting the same disease, he felt like he could handle it better because he was older, because he understood. But for those young ones, it was simply unfair.

"Puss and Boots" and reporter from the Detroit
News interviewing David *Photo credit for
Todd McInturf/The Detroit News*

By that weekend, David was heading home. Only one more round of methotrexate and that stage of chemotherapy would be over. He had ten days to recover, to feel stronger before going back to the hospital. In the meantime, on Friday, October 21, 2011, the Detroit Red Wings were playing the Columbus Blue Jackets and David was planning on attending. Not only was he planning on watching the Red Wings, but he was planning on shoveling for them. David received clearance from his doctors but was instructed not to overexert himself. Even Al, the building operations manager and Zamboni driver for the Red Wings, suggested to David that he not skate all around the ice but rather shovel just one area. Al loved David and didn't want him taxing himself but was elated to have him back for the evening, and what an evening it was, as that hockey game just happened to be dedicated to cancer awareness.

> Friday night is hockey fights cancer night at Joe Louis! It's gonna be a teary night.
> —David Mannino,
> October 19, 2011, Facebook post

Tom and I decided to go down to the Joe that night to watch the game and see David shovel. I felt more comfortable being at the arena, with David there, than being at home, should he not feel well. I could tell that he didn't have quite the energy as usual, but it was awesome to see David step back on the ice with his friends, dressed in his Red Wings attire, something he absolutely loved. It was such a positive and enjoyable change of environment for him as it gave him a chance to forget that on Monday, bright and early, the final round of methotrexate would begin.

> Back to the hospital.
> —David Mannino,
> October 24, 2011, Facebook post

As I watched David journey through a cancer diagnosis, I watched a boy grow into a man. Cancer, which meant to destroy, became the means by which that boy grew spiritually and developed a mature, Christ-centered faith. God was leading that journey, and

His purposes would be fulfilled. The following statement was by far David's most profound Facebook post.

> How will you live your life? There are two choices, either for God or against Him. The beautiful thing is that it is our choice, but with such a choice comes risks and rewards. There is no wavering in between or picking and choosing aspects of each to create your own way of living. It's simple— you either choose to or choose not to, and if you choose God, the battle has only begun because then you must live the unpopular and anti-societal way of living. Yet no matter how badly you are chastised because of this way of living, remember that through this and through Christ comes a first-class ticket to salvation. God doesn't put or destine you to hell. It's *your* own choice. The time is now, not tomorrow or when it becomes easy for you, because life is short and never easy, and you will never have the ability to live without Him. Go ahead and try it by yourself. Sadly, you'll find a dead end. For me the choice is simple, so I implore everyone who reads this to push away your fears, insecurities, and pride and give your life to the Lord. Life is simply an audition for determining where you will spend eternity, and funny thing is *you* get to choose by how you and for whom you live your life. So, I ask again, how will you live your life? I choose to bring it!
>
> —David Mannino,
> October 26, 2011, Facebook post

The final round of methotrexate was completed with no additional issues, and David was counting down to the homestretch.

Phase 3 is completed. One more two-month phase of misery ahead and then a year of maintenance. Going home! Thanks be to God!

—David Mannino,
October 27, 2011, Facebook post

Chapter 23

David had ten days to recover before stage 4—delayed intensification—would begin. As mentioned previously, this would be the knockout punch for lymphoma. Any possible remnant of a cancer cell would hopefully be eliminated. I couldn't even imagine that there could be any remnants left. After all the agonizing chemotherapy already administered, how could there possibly be even the tiniest of cancer cells remaining? It almost seemed unrealistic.

> It all starts back up now. Two more months of an intense battle. Need those prayers!
>
> —David Mannino,
> November 7, 2011, Facebook post

> Bringing it!
>
> —David Mannino,
> November 7, 2011, Facebook post

David forged ahead, knowing that the end was in sight, but the chemotherapy was unrelenting and took a toll on his body. His blood counts were in a constant state of abnormality, and once again blood transfusions were needed. The long process of transfusions began.

> Lord, just please get me through this day.
>> —David Mannino,
>> November 11, 2011, Facebook post

The blood transfusions went well, without event, and David was once again looking forward to going home, because within three short days he would return to continue the course. It occurred to me that this battle produced the constant desire for the simple things in life, things you take for granted … *home!*

> Back to the hospital. Bringing it time!
>> —David Mannino,
>> November 14, 2011, Facebook post

Stage 4 was then in full force, just as challenging as the three previous stages. David kept his focus on the new year and his plans for the future. By mid-January he was to begin the maintenance stage, and by April he would have finally begun his freshman year at the University of Michigan.

> Only through Him.
>> —David Mannino,
>> November 15, 2011, Facebook post

> Thank the Lord!
>> —David Mannino,
>> November 20, 2011, Facebook post

> Chase greatness and thank the Lord while achieving it.
>> —David Mannino,
>> November 22, 2011, Facebook post

Thanksgiving was only a few days away. Originally David wanted a quiet Thanksgiving with just the five of us because he was feeling exhausted and battered from all the treatment. But as the week progressed, David changed his mind. A couple of days prior to Thanksgiving, David decided that spending that day with extended family as well as with his immediate family would be more gratifying. Therefore, we spent the holiday with relatives, but David was very serene that night. That charismatic, spirited personality was simply quieted. Clearly the chemotherapy was silently rearing its effects. The next day David remained very lowkey. Three of his closest friends came over to see him as they were home from college for the Thanksgiving break. It felt so normal, so great, to have David's friends visiting. It started to feel like old times again, before the diagnosis. Oh, how I relished those days, months, even years, before we learned of his cancer diagnosis. If only I could go back and embrace each moment and hold onto each day when life was free from complication and suffering. His friends stayed for most of the day and even had dinner with us, but I could tell that David was simply not himself. After we ate dinner and his friends left, David went to bed. He was feeling tired, and it was quite evident. By the next morning, Saturday, November 26, David woke up and came downstairs only to inform me that he wasn't feeling well. Something felt different! David had abdominal pains that did not resemble anything he had previously experienced. I quickly reached for my phone and dialed the doctor. We were instructed to take David to the ER.

> Going to the emergency room.
> —David Mannino,
> November 26, 2011, final Facebook post

By the time we arrived at the ER, David was buckled over in pain. After a series of tests taken, the diagnosis was clear. David was suffering from an acute pancreatitis, brought on by an extremely rare reaction from one of the chemotherapy drugs that had been administered two weeks prior. This reaction presents with little warning and carries a poor prognosis. Such a reaction can be catastrophic and irreversible!

Through all the discomfort David was unable to verbally communicate. But he conveyed one final thought—one final lesson—to me. He raised his arm in the air and pointed toward heaven.

I looked at him and asked him, "Are you trying to tell me that God is in control?" He looked at me and nodded ... *yes!* David inspired me until the end. On Monday, November 28, in spite of all the medical attention given, due to complications, David passed away into the loving arms of his Savior.

> I have fought the good fight, I have finished the race, I have kept the faith. (2 Timothy 4:7)

> "For my thoughts are not your thoughts, neither are your ways my ways," declares the Lord. "As the heavens are higher than the earth, so are my ways higher than your ways and my thoughts than your thoughts." (Isaiah 55:8–9)

Chapter 24

David's faith was pure. It wasn't conditional or based only on fulfilled desires. David ran the race to win, and winning is what he accomplished. David achieved his ultimate goal: eternal salvation. David's favorite song by the group Coldplay was "Paradise," a place that he now fully understands. David taught me how to trust God even though my reasoning may not be God's reasoning. God gave David an assignment on May 3, 2011, and David completed the assignment on November 28, 2011. I will never understand God's ways, nor would I have chosen this journey, but God sees the entire picture, while I see only one frame.

> The secret things belong to the Lord our God.
> (Deuteronomy 29:29)

There are no words to adequately describe the pain and suffering associated with losing a child. However, through a tremendous amount of prayer and devotion over these past seven years, God has shown me His hand of grace and has taught me that He is sovereign. God has always been in control! Through *all* pain and suffering there is an eternal purpose!

> Mothers who lose children … are broken!
> Mothers who lose children … are encased in profound grief!

Mothers who lose children ... feel abandoned!
Mothers who lose children ... struggle to breathe!
Mothers who lose children ... question tomorrow!

However, with Christ:

Mothers who lose children, who trust Christ ... will heal!
Mothers who lose children, who trust Christ ... will feel the hand of God pick them up and carry them through!
Mothers who lose children, who trust Christ ... will be enveloped by God's loving arms, and He will breathe for them!
Mothers who lose children, who trust Christ ... will experience joy again!
Mothers who lose children, who trust Christ ... will hold their child again!

> He gives strength to the weary and increases the power of the weak. Even youths grow tired and weary, and young men stumble and fall; but those who hope in the Lord will renew their strength. They will soar on wings like eagles; they will run and not grow weary, they will walk and not be faint. (Isaiah 40:29–31)

On November 28, 2011, God allowed David's voice to be silenced, but God also allowed his legacy to resonate forever.

> He will wipe every tear from their eyes. There will be no more death or mourning or crying or pain, for the old order of things has passed away. (Revelation 21:4)

Thoughts and Memories

I didn't know David very long, but in the short time that I did, I knew he made an impression and left a beautiful footprint on this earth ... He believed, maybe a little more than the rest of us, a little harder, and a little stronger ... I believe he is at peace now ... It is a journey he was prepared for. David, you will never be forgotten.

—Lexi

The world and I lost a fine young man ... David Mannino. He was eighteen years old. I only knew David for a few months, but the few hours that I spoke with him left me so impressed and inspired by his courage and faith. I met him a few months back at a Tigers/Yankees playoff game. He was there with his father and me with my son. We were sitting together, and as the game progressed, we began to talk about the game and sports in general. As the conversation moved along, he told me that he worked at Joe Louis for the Red Wings. I asked him what he did, and he told me that he was part of the ice cleaning crew that skated out during TV time outs and shoveled off the excess snow. When he said that, I immediately recognized him as he was always at the end of the rink where our seats are located.

I said, "I recognize you now. You are the tall young man with the big head of black hair."

He laughed and said, "That's me, but I was just diagnosed with leukemia."

My heart sank, but in that very moment he looked at me and said with a huge smile, "But I am doing much better and I will beat this through prayer and faith." The baseball game seemed of little importance anymore.

We continued to talk about his love of UM and how he was supposed to be attending school there but could not because of his treatment, but again he lit up and said he would be there next year. He told me every stat there was about UM sports and how much better the football team was going to be this year. I bet he was proud of them. He talked about his father and how they did things. He told me that this was the first time he had been out in some time because of his treatments and the risk of infection. He laughed after he shook someone's hand that his dad told him to go wash his hands. The rest of the night was filled with more conversation and laughter about nothing in particular but very enjoyable.

He said, "Take my number and when you are at a Red Wings game I will bring you down to where they stand." We exchanged numbers and looked forward to seeing each other at the game.

The Tiger game came to an end. We were surprised at that as we were only partially paying attention. The evening seemed to come to an end that neither of us wanted as conversation seemed to just keep rolling along. We all shook hands. I told him that we would be thinking of him in our thoughts and prayers.

He replied again with a big smile, "I will be better. It's all about prayer and faith."

We walked up the stairs and headed our own ways. A few months later, I was at one of the early-season Red Wings games with my wife. I said to her, "I wonder if David is working the ice tonight."

During the next timeout I looked up and there he was just working a small area, but he was out there. After they got off the ice, I texted him to say hello. He responded and wanted to know where I was sitting. I stood up and waved like a crazy person hoping that he could see me, not certain if he ever did, but we texted some more and then said talk later.

To my sadness, I did not communicate enough after that with him.

But the night before Thanksgiving I was at the Wings game with my father, my son, and a friend of my sons. I was talking with my father when the kids came out to clean the ice and I looked to see if David was there, but he was not. I told my father the story of meeting David and then decided to try to text him. I said hello and asked if he was at the game. He replied immediately with a hello but that he was not at the game.

He said that he was going through a difficult treatment so he could not be there, but he said, "I will see you there in January." We exchanged some additional text messages. He thanked me for contacting him and said, "You have a great holiday, and see you soon." I so wish that I would have called him rather than texted. I told him, "Keep the faith and believe as I believe in you."

Yesterday I received a call from my wife at work. She told me that our daughter had just texted her from school saying that David had passed away on Monday and didn't I know him. I felt as though my own family had been lost. My life is so much richer to have known David even if it was only for a few hours at a game and some text messages. His faith and belief inspire me and touched my life just as I am certain it touched so many others. This world has lost so much with his passing. Those who knew him have lost so much, and those who did not know him have missed so much. People say there is a plan when these things happen. I am struggling with what that plan could possibly be. He was a young man so full of life, with so much to offer, so many things to accomplish and conquer, taken so very young from his family, his friends, and the world. I have known David for such a short time, yet I feel this great loss of a lifelong friend. I can't bring myself to come to terms with this at all. Our daughter who did not know David but has seen all the social messaging about him sent me a note last night saying how much she loved and appreciated her family. We just had Thanksgiving together, the time to give thanks for what we all have and be with those we love as well as extending that to others.

Love those around you. Reach out to those you know and offer help or support. Be aware of what you have and not what we want. Life is so very short and can be so cruel. We all have so much to be thankful for each and every moment of every day. Be certain to tell those and cherish those around you all the moments of your life.

> Rest in peace, David. Thank you so very much.
> You will be missed by all.
>
> —Craig W.

The English language lacks the words necessary to describe how truly special of a human being David was. I feel any attempt I give to try and match words to his character will be all but an utter failure. Nevertheless, David was one of my closest and dearest friends, so I have an immense desire to try to capture his immeasurable spirit. During one of my visits to see Dave in the hospital this summer, I had a truly memorable conversation with him. James and I had been chilling in his hospital room for a while when suddenly David asked James to leave so he could talk to me alone. James complied, and I curiously went over and sat on the bed with Dave. For over a half an hour, while James wandered the hospital's hallways, David gave me advice on the relationship I had just gotten out of and many other aspects of my life that were troubling me. The details of what we talked about doesn't matter. What matters is the fact that even though David was being pumped with poison, he still took the time to make sure that I was okay. He was suffering from cancer, and what he cared about was giving me advice and letting me know that he was there to talk to whenever and about whatever.

I had yet another memorable conversation with Dave. Unfortunately, it was only over texting, exactly two weeks before he died. I was telling him that I would be home for Thanksgiving soon and that he better stop being stubborn and let me see him. Once the chemo treatment started to take a bigger toll on his body, he had become resistant to letting me visit because he didn't want me to see him "weak." He was always so concerned about not freaking me out or stopping me from worrying about him. Little did he know, I saw right through the act. And me not worry about him? Ha, that's funny … Anyway, during this conversation he texted me, "Menial things are worthless. Life is about family, God, and health. That's it, girl." Leave it to David to send me meaningful, beautiful words out of the blue. He had such an amazing outlook on life and constantly pushed me to see things through his eyes.

The stories are endless, the memories unforgettable. However, I want to end this by saying I loved David and feel nothing but blessed to have considered him a best friend. Although it sounds cliché,

99

being his friend has made me a better person and I wouldn't be who I am today without the influence he had on my life. He will be forever missed and never forgotten.

—Samantha W.

As a young high schooler, trying to find your place and make a positive impression on those around you is a confusing and difficult time in any person's life. Being different, doing what is right, and most importantly not caring if people looked at you differently because of your decisions is a balancing act that most high school kids fail at.

Simply being around Dave and watching him make unpopular but positive decisions helped form me as a young man. Dave was unapologetically goofy, sometimes arrogant, and most importantly, always honest. Whether he was lecturing me on the dangers of chewing tobacco on our rides home from hockey or telling me about how he doesn't talk to very many girls because of his fear they would hinder his perfectly planned out future, he never batted an eye when someone told him to live a little or take another perspective.

Dave taught me that people give advice all the time. They try to give you tips and tricks to improve yourself, but we get tired of hearing that. On our car rides home from our Detroit ice rink to our cushy suburban homes, we would play heartfelt songs much too loud and just listen. Most likely we were thinking of different things. I was probably thinking about a high school girlfriend, and he was most likely thinking of his future of becoming a doctor. Those parts of our worlds never did end up colliding, but he helped me find inspiration and thoughtfulness in simply enjoying a great song with a better friend … Dave taught me that sometimes a friend can lift you up by being there in the passenger seat, and a song can help you envision a bright future while enjoying the present.

> I'm thankful for him and that lesson every time I find myself in those peaceful moments. Where I know that even if I'm alone, Dave is there in the passenger seat pushing me in the right direction.
> —Oscar Mansky

Oscar and David, curling in Calumet,
Michigan (February 2011)

The two things that struck me about David in high school are the same things that strike me even more profoundly as I grow: his ability to connect with everybody on a real level and his unmatched confidence. I think the two go hand in hand. 1) His ability to connect with anybody. Whether it was talking to a superior, like a teacher, or somebody much younger, like the ten younger hockey players that Dave always had following him around, he saw people as equals on our journey through life. Of course, this got him in trouble from time to time, but the majority of the time it created a connection between Dave and whoever he was with. Nobody had relationships with the U of D staff, teachers, coaches, or lunch ladies like David did. 2) Dave's unmatched confidence. It's something I try to embody in myself every day. Dave was authentically himself. In an eighteen-year-old, that's almost unheard of. This also got him into trouble from time to time ... But that authenticity brought him confidence to be who he was and stick by what he thought was right. The last thing I'll say is how incredible this was at such a young age. These are qualities that most in their twenties, thirties, and beyond struggle with, yet David at eighteen possessed the characteristics of a man. David was a role model to me in high school and that same eighteen-year-old is who I look to for guidance today, seven years after he's passed.

—Walter Mansky

Walter and David, Cranbrook Ice Arena,
Bloomfield Hills, Michigan, sporting the
Olde English D, Summer hockey 2010

David Mannino was an extraordinary young
man. Our son, Tyler, played with David on the
Little Caesars AAA hockey team. David was a
big, strong power forward, and he could really
play the game. He also had a personality that
was very intoxicating, making him extremely
popular. He was so genuine and raw, and it was
hard not to love him. I remember talking with
David about the Lord and David's faith in Jesus,
even before he knew he had cancer. I remember
thinking how mature his relationship with Christ
was considering he was still a teenager. David

and I quickly became close friends, and as we learned of his cancer, our conversations about faith and God's plan became more frequent. My wife and I often talk about how this young man touched so many lives. Everyone knew of David and that he was a true believer. I look back at the example he set, for each of us at the Detroit Red Wings, Little Caesar AAA Hockey, Olympia Entertainment, and U of D Jesuit. These are just a few of the communities that David touched. We feel blessed to have known this young man and truly appreciate the example that he set.

—Glenn Murray and Lisa Ilitch Murray

If you wish to contact the author, please
use the following email address.
annita@bringit22.org
or
visit the website:
www.bringit22.org
All proceeds from this book go to the
David Mannino Foundation Inc.

CPSIA information can be obtained
at www.ICGtesting.com
Printed in the USA
LVHW090019191118
597596LV00006B/29/P

9 781973 639893